# Fortnite For Teens

## *Advanced Tips, Tricks and Strategies To Help You Win #1 Victory Royale EVERYTIME!*

*By*

**Elite Gamer Guides**

## *Elite Gamer Guides*

hardship or damages that may befall them after undertaking information described herein.

Additionally, the information in the following pages is intended only for informational purposes and should thus be thought of as universal. As befitting its nature, it is presented without assurance regarding its prolonged validity or interim quality. Trademarks that are mentioned are done without written consent and can in no way be considered an endorsement from the trademark holder.

# Table of Contents

# **Introduction**

Congratulations on purchasing this book and welcome to the world of Fortnite. Fortnite: Battle Royale is the game that the entire world is talking about. It is n online battle royale game that consists of a hundred players battling it out until the last man standing. The game is high paced, action packed, and most of all, absolutely fun. You can collect fancy outfits and skins to make your characters look both funky and weird.

*The aim of this strategy book is to adjust your mindset so that you will be ready to take on all of the challenges and obstacles associated with the game.*

The Fortnite Battle Royale mode is very different from most shooters that require you to go for max kills in order to win. In Fortnite, you need to fight and build your way to survival.

This book also aims to have you playing the game like the pros. The tips and tricks in this book can quickly assist you in adapting a playing style that is similar to the pros who are famous for playing Fortnite.

I'm sure you enjoy reading this book as much as you would enjoy playing Fortnite. The best way to understand the tips here is to put it into practice by playing the game. Always remember that you will be up against other players that have already dedicated plenty off hours towards mastering their skill. It will take you time to get there as well. In doing so, always remember that it is just a game and you should always try to have fun first.

# Chapter 1: Winning PUBG Vs. Fortnite

Fortnite: Battle Royale is based on the now popular battle royale mode which places 100 players into an open world map where they will battle it out till the last man standing. Gameplay in the map is restricted to a specific yet random area which is highlighted by a circle on the map. If a player remains outside that circle, they will begin to critically lose health. This forces players to move towards an area that will potentially have other players that they will need to battle.

This battle royale concept has been around for some time now. But only recently has this mode gained worldwide attention. **One of the most recent games to popularize the battle royale concept is Player Unknown's Battlegrounds (PUBG).** PUBG is one of the top 10 selling games of all time. Part of its success is its fresh take on the shooter genre.

Most shooter games have a similar premise and gaming style attached to it, which is usually all about getting the most kills. PUBG, on the other hand, is about surviving until the end.

**Epic Games Fortnite enters the Battle Royale genre with a slightly different take on the gameplay and graphics. Unlike PUBG's more realistic styling and gameplay, Fortnite maintains its cartoonish graphics while introducing its building mechanics to the battle royale mode. This makes Fortnite: Battle Royale unique in its own way while adding layers of functionality to the game. The ability to build walls and stairs to shelter you from unsuspected attackers allows you to play Fortnite in a very different way than you would play PUBG.**

You would still have to land on the map and loot items such as weapons and health. But in Fortnite you will also have to harvest materials such as wood, brick, and metal in order to construct various buildings and ramps. You can even go big and build yourself a massive fort. This ability makes for a more customized approach to the game. You don't have to be restricted to the pathways and roads set on a map. You can build your own ramps and stairs up hills, cliffs, and even buildings.

**The one major thing that a PUBG player will have to learn to get used to is the overall lighthearted nature of the Fortnite series.** Besides its cartoonish graphics and arcade-style gameplay, Fortnite has other campy elements to it such as dropping dance moves, outrageous costumes, and weird game modes. This makes for a fun experience that transfers over to the Fortnite community of players who enjoy dance competitions and special events centered around the wacky antics of the game.

# Chapter 2: Tips from Pros- Build Strong

There are three games modes to choose from in the main game menu. Namely, Solo (just you against 99 other people), Duo (play with a teammate), and Squad modes (play along with three other players in a squad). After selecting the mode you wish to play, you will then start off in a pre-game lobby area where you can do a small bit of exploring before the game starts. Then you and the rest of the players will be transported towards the map in a battle bus that is suspended high in the air by a hot air balloon.

After being ejected from the battle bus, you will be in a free fall state until you decide to activate your glider (automatically activates when close to the ground). While free falling, you can control your avatar by moving them around. This will allow you to guide yourself to a specific point on the map, as well as fall faster. It's advisable to free fall down as fast as possible before automatically activating the glider. This way you reach the ground as quickly as possible. Activating the glider early will leave you hovering in the sky for quite some time.

It's important to remember that you will eject out of the battle bus along with another 99 players. This means that there is a possibility that plenty of you will fall towards similar landing spots. If this happens, then you will have to rush and loot weapons alongside an opponent. When you do find something, then you will have to attack or defend yourself immediately from the nearby threat.

This may seem like an exciting scenario, to rush out, loot, and attack. But it gets old quickly as the chances of someone ending your game in this scenario is really high. The name of the game is survival after all. It's best to avoid these busy areas early on. Rather glide over to an area on the map that doesn't have too many opponents nearby. Landing in towns and other areas with plenty of buildings can increase your chances of receiving good loot, but it also increases your chances of having to engage in combat with someone.

# Surviving the First Minute

It is possible to find landing spots away from other players. One way to do this is to eject as late as possible. Most people will already be on the ground while you are just about to eject. But you will be able to avoid these people while landing in a safer area away from them. This is an ideal tactic for those looking to pull off stealthier victories. This way you can sneak your way around the map away from other opponents while you loot and harvest.

**It is important to remember that stealth and patience are absolutely vital here. Especially when taking the stealth route. Move around as quietly as possible while constantly remaining hidden. If you do come across other players, don't engage. Instead, move into an area away from the**

**gunfire. It's better to just allow the other players to take each other out.**

You can monitor other peoples battles carefully in the distance and only engage once there is just one person left. But it isn't advisable to do so. There's still a possibility of someone attacking you while you watch others. It's best to only defend yourself when someone jumps out to attack you.

# Chapter 3: Get Unlimited V-Bucks Rewards

V-Bucks is the Fortnite in-game currency. You can use V-Bucks to purchase all kinds of goodies from skins to outfits to emotes. You can even use your V-Bucks to buy a Battle Pass which can also be used to unlock more items. The Battle Pass is a tiered system that runs during a season. It can help you unlock challenges in which you can earn more items.

The most simple way to get V-Bucks is to log into the game every day. A daily login will earn you a daily reward. Each day is a chance of that daily reward being V-Bucks. Completing daily and weekly quests will give you the opportunity to earn rewards such as Survivors, Heroes, Schematics, and V-Bucks. It is possible to complete at least one quest in a day that has a V-Bucks reward attached to it. This is why quests are advisable if you wish to earn V-Bucks.

You can also earn V-Bucks by adding items such as schematics and weapons into the Collection Book. Adding items here will give you experience for the Collection Book which can level. Once you do level up, you will receive a reward. In most cases it is V-Bucks. It is important to note that once you add items to the Collection Book, they will be permanently gone.

If you require V-Bucks urgently, you can just simply opt to buy V-Bucks using your own real hard earned cash. There will be times when you urgently require a specific costume or item. Completing quests for V-Bucks will take too long and the offer for the item will expire or it will not be available anymore. This is when you should rather just use some of your cash to buy V-Bucks so that you don't miss out. Epic Games has put in a lot of effort behind releasing this free game. Any cash you spend is well deserved by them.

# Chapter 4: Ultimate Tips for Landing, Looting, Harvesting and Weapons

## 1. Landing

The way you start off your battle royale can make or break the current session that you are in. You can choose to either eject early in order to be among the first few to land or you can wait and eject late for a more stealthier approach. Landing early will allow you to be among the first few to begin looting. This can be the perfect opportunity to acquire weapons before anyone else. You can already start attacking your opponents as they begin to land.

The downside to this strategy is that you could land in an area that is already filled up with other players who are on a looting craze. You will most probably run into other players as you are getting your looting. It's best to be really quick here if you want to survive. It's also important to remember not to land in a spot where someone else is already looting. They could already be armed as you are bracing yourself to land.

People who want to play a quite campaign can opt to land later on. This way, you can land in the distance away from the rest of the pack. Make sure you land in a secluded spot slightly away from buildings. People tend to hideout in buildings and snipe. Rather aim for a spot that has places like trees and hills for cover. You can move on gradually from here towards smaller houses and buildings and begin looting.

## 2. Looting

Looting is crucial if you wish to create an effective offense. Consistently being on the move as you pass through areas with weapons will increase your chance of finding a powerful weapon. Looting in areas that already have a few opponents means two things, they could have already taken the best weapons, you will possibly engage with them.

A great way to recover some valuable weapons is to loot opponents that you have already taken out. After defeating another player, all their items will be scattered around for you to go and collect. But be aware as this means that you will be left vulnerable in an area for others to lock onto you. Make sure that area is secure before you go in and browse the available weapons.

This tactic runs two ways as you could snipe in the distance and watch other players engage and defeat each other. Wait for a player to take out another and let him approach the defeated players loot. At this moment, they will be stationary for a short while. This is when you can line up a critical shot out in the distance.

## 3. Harvesting

Destroying items in Fortnite with your pickaxe will allow you to harvest valuable building materials such as wood, brick, and metal. Almost any item in the game can be destroyed. But focusing on a single item and hitting it until it is destroyed is not advisable. Hitting these items creates noise which can give away your position. Certain items such as large trees can be seen moving when destroyed. Even from the distance.

It's best to constantly be on the move when harvesting, so if someone Is nearby, they won't be able to lock onto you. Keep hitting objects only a few times then move to the next one. You don't have to fully destroy objects. You can also increase the number of materials that you harvest by aiming towards the center of the red target as you hit objects. This is the sweet spot that allows you to destroy items faster while collecting more materials. Keep on the move while hitting items at the center of the red target.

Harvesting inside a house is another great way to collect all kinds of materials quickly. You can get bricks from walls, wood from furniture, and metal from stoves or fridges. This makes for a productive and safe way to harvest. Just get into an empty home and demolish everything in sight!

# 4. Weapons

Your weapon inventory is restricted as you can only carry a few weapons with you. So make sure that you have the right ones at all times. Fortnite has probably the largest selection of weapons ever seen in a game. But not all weapons are amazing in Battle Royale mode. It's best to stick to a few effective weapons during a campaign.

Shotguns, pistols, and SMGs are great, but they are difficult to use in an offense in Battle Royale mode. There will be a lot of battles that take place in the distance. Weapons such as assault and sniper rifles are great in these scenarios. Because of the nature of the game, you will be moving around the map a lot in order to get to the center of the circle. This is when you will come across other players as you move around. It's best to engage these people only from a distance.

Assault rifles are excellent as they are just as effective in close range combat. The only downside to these weapons is that they tend to have some recoil. Constantly holding the "fire" button down will send the rifle into an automatic frenzy. When this happens, then accuracy is thrown out of the window as the aiming bloom widens and bullets are just sprayed all over the place and not at the center of the target.

## 5. Treasure Chests

You can find treasure chests in some buildings. One of the things that you will find in them is weapons. You may not be able to see these treasure chests immediately, but you will be able to hear them. They give off a light shimmering sound which gives you an indication that they are nearby. Keep heading in the direction of the sound to find the treasure chest. Even if it means you breaking down the walls to do so.

# Chapter 5: Advanced Tips and Tricks

We have already discussed some important tips and tricks as to how to quickly become successful in Fortnite: Battle Royale. In this chapter, we will quickly summarize the most important aspects behind achieving a victory in the game. You can use this chapter as a quick reference while achieving victory in the game yourself.

1. Master your landing

2. Memorize locations

3. Harvest on the move

4. Build as you are attacked

5. Movement

6. High ground

7. Don't plan on taking out everyone

8. Build a base and fight to win

# 1. Master Your Landing

Always aim for areas that are free from other players. Landing next to a building that is occupied by an opponent increases the chances of that opponent jumping you before you even begin to loot. It's better to land off in the distance away from all of the action. Even if there aren't too many places to loot. You can always sneak on over to a vacant building in the distance to begin looting.

But you can't help but defend yourself if you are competing for weapons in a building that has two or more opponents that are looting. This scenario decreases your chances of survival in the battle royale mode. An excellent way to make sure you land away from the action is to eject yourself from the battle bus really late. Allowing the bus to travel further will also move you further away from players who instantly jump off the bus at the start.

## 2. Memorize Locations

Memorizing locations is considered to be a great tactic in Fortnite Battle Royale. Not only will you be really familiar with the landscape and its buildings, but you will also have a good idea of the spawn locations of chests. You don't have to memorize the entire map. Just focus on a few areas and try to learn the ins and outs of these places well. This will also help you when choosing a place to land.

## 3. Harvest on the Move

Never stay in one place for too long. Especially when harvesting. Repeatedly hitting a single object while standing still can turn you into an easy target. Even fully destroying a large object like a tree can alert other players from a distance. It's best to keep on the move and hit items only a few times and then continue moving. This way you get your materials while moving towards your destination and also avoiding any close by attackers.

# 4. Build As You Are Attacked

Make use of Fortnite's revolutionary building system. The ability to instantly start building a defense around you as people are attacking is an amazing feature that doesn't exist in other shooters. The ability to think fast and build quickly and effectively can save you from defeat. You can take a perilous situation and turn it around by building a defense that leads to higher ground. Speed is key here.

# 5. Movement

You will do plenty of traveling in this game as you try to make it to the center of the circle. Always remember Not to move in a straight line towards your destination. This makes you an easy and predictable target for other players, especially snipers. Try to adopt a different approach and mentality when moving around in this game. You can do this by constantly running and jumping into opposing directions whilst heading towards your destination.

# 6. High Ground

It's always important to maintain the high ground, especially late in the game. Build simple yet effective structures that can easily place you higher than your opponents. Building a ramp that leads to a wall can make plenty of difference on a flat surface. When an opponent approaches you, all they will see is the wall, you, on the other hand, will be able to move up the ramp on the other side and can quickly pop your head out the top and attack.

# 7. Don't Plan on Taking Out Everyone

The key to victory in Fortnite is survival. Attacking other players seriously weakens your odds for survival. It's best to just let people run off and fight each other than you hunting every person you come across. If you do notice someone in the distance, its best to wait until you have a critical shot. Shooting them and missing will only alert them. This will lead to them attacking you.

# 8. Build a Base and Fight to Win

Build a base in order to keep safe towards the end of a game. You may be required to abandon your base so you can move to the center of the circle. In this case, build another while ensuring that you have the high ground. Again, patience is key here so you will need a strong and well-designed base in order to hold off attacks. The base doesn't have to be really fancy, just good enough to defend yourself.

# Chapter 6: Inventory and Play Style

In Fortnite: Battle Royale you are equipped with a default inventory system. There are five slots that you can use to store weapons, meds, grenades, and other gear. There are separate slots for building materials. You will find your pickaxe at quick selection number 1. This is the main weapon that you will use to harvest and it will continue to stay here.

Once you have looted and acquired weapons, you will be able to modify them by placing them in quick access slots. It's is possible to also drop and share items that you have when in duo or team mode. This is useful if you wish to assist teammates that are low on inventory.

Placing weapons in slots that correspond to your favorite hotkeys can assist you in efficiently drawing out your weapon of choice. An example would be to have slot one for an assault rifle and slot two for a sniper. All you have to do is tap the corresponding hockey for slot two to equip yourself quickly with a sniper.

## Rarity and DPS

In Fortnite there is an item class system that helps you to differentiate between the different weapons and items. Common weapons are standard variants of a particular gun such as an assault rifle. Uncommon, rare, epic and legendary assault rifles have improved abilities such as DPS that are better than a common assault rifle. This goes for the rest of the weapons, such as snipers, pistols, and SMG's.

DPS (damage per second) is calculated by multiplying a weapons damage with its fire rate. When comparing weapons, DPS isn't the measurement you should always trust, especially if you are comparing assault rifles with shotguns.

A shotgun can have a higher damage statistic,

but its fire rate is really low. Because of this, the DPS goes low too. The same goes for sniper rifles that can take out opponents with one or two shots. They cause an insane amount of damage but have really slow reload speeds. This brings the DPS right down.

It's best to stick to the right weapons for the right occasions. Shotguns for close combat, and snipers for long distance fights. Whatever the case may be, rarity still plays a huge role as legendary and epic weapons are the right weapons to keep in your inventory.

# Choosing the Right Weapon

The weapons in Fortnite are based on real-life counterparts. But they do however have an arcade feel to them. Repetitive gunfire can cause bullets to continuously spray in all directions. Especially with automatic assault rifles. It's best to shoot in short bursts. This helps to keep the gun steady and will help you master assault rifles quickly.

Every weapon in Fortnite may be fun to use, but not all are effective. There are major advantages in using assault and sniper rifles. You obviously cannot select these weapons at the start. You will be required to loot in order to come across them. When you do, it's advisable to keep them. You will be engaging in plenty of long-range battles. This is when snipers and assault rifles will be useful.

An added bonus is that assault rifles are just as good within close range. Shotguns are also good in close range combat. Their downfall is their slow reload times.

## Mindset and Movement

Fortnite: Battle Royale is in no way an ordinary third-person shooter. The game has all these extra elements that form to create a uniquely enjoyable experience. You will be required to play this game differently.

Traditional shooter games have taught us how to respond and react to these type of games. But with Fortnite, you will have to change your mindset.

There are just a few things that you will need to remember when adjusting to a mindset that is in line with Fortnite.

- Be super alert

- Be quick

- Build quick

- Outmaneuver and outbuild opponents

- Always be on the move

- Harvest

- Survive

When you begin to focus and master these

aspects of the game, you will notice that you will develop a new mindset that is associated with shooter games. Older games required you to kill as many opponents as possible in order to earn the most points. Killing doesn't matter in Fortnite, it's all about survival. You will need to perfect your movement and building in order to survive.

Be sneaky at all times or when you can. Using sound to your advantage is the way to go. It is recommended to play Fortnite with headphones. This way you could listen for nearby gunfights or footsteps. If you do hear someone approaching, try to position yourself away from their site if possible. Only engage when you have to. It's best to just wait and as everyone kills each other. Then you can plan an attack on the last person left.

Always try your best to avoid death at all times. Do not play the game to achieve maximum kills. This can be very risky because you will be spending most of your time in gunfights. This will drastically decrease your chances of survival. Don't be the hero that runs towards enemies to gun them down. Never underestimate the skill of the next player. They are not AI characters, instead of human online gamers that have put in endless hours into the game.

# Chapter 7: The Secret Building Strategy That No One Wants You To Know

One of the biggest elements of the Fortnite franchise is the ability to build. You will have to learn to focus partly on harvesting materials in order to rebuild structures and forts which can be used to defend yourself. You can also build ramps that can allow you to access higher ground or other buildings and forts.

Fortnite has a simple, yet effective grid-based building system. At first use, it may seem difficult to build, but the mechanics behind building in Fortnite isn't that difficult to understand. Even basic building can open up new tactical possibilities. The simple controls allow you to improvise mid-battle as you build walls to defend yourself or stairs leading up a hill away from gunfire.

# Materials

Building in Fortnite also allows you to create custom forts. You can go for a basic design or really get creative by building a huge castle. But you can only accomplish this by using building materials such as Wood, Brick, and Metal. Each material has its own set of pros and cons. Using wood to build is the quickest way to get any structure up. But wood is also the weakest material with a health rating of 200. Wood structures can easily be taken down my opponents who can simply shoot through them.

Metal takes the most time to construct, but it is the strongest having a health rating of 400. A fully built metal structure could possibly withstand a single RPG or grenade attack. Constant attack opens a metal structure will eventually bring it down. You can use the time an opponent takes to destroy your metal fort to regroup and reposition yourself. This is why metal is a good choice for building bases and forts towards the end of a game. Brick is right in between wood and metal, taking more time to construct than wood, but less time than metal. Brick has a health rating of 300.

Wood is best used during combat situations because it is the quickest to build. If you wish to build as you fight, then you should consider harvesting as much wood as possible. Also, don't forget to preselect wood in the building menu. This makes it quicker and easier to initiate building a wood structure that can serve as a line of defense to unsuspected attackers. If your menu is preselected on metal, then you could drop a metal wall by mistake which will be of no use while being attacked. This is due to its slow-building quality.

Bricks take longer to build than wood but are stronger. These are great for building short-term forts that you can use to heal yourself. You can also use the brick material to build stairs in situations when you are not in danger. This is a good way to conserve wood for the more dangerous situations.

# Use Building to Defend Yourself

Building strong forts is a great way to camp out while the rest of the players battle it out. The downside to this is that other players will be able to easily spot your building. It won't be long until they figure out that you are hiding in there. If someone sees your building in the middle of nowhere, they might just have the guts to approach it and try to take you out. In this case, you should hope that they are not armed with an RPG. Always expect the worst in situations like this and make sure you are prepared.

Every millisecond counts when building. The speed at which you can build your defenses and escape routes can determine your success in Fortnite. It is possible to remap your building keys (on PC) closer to your A-S-D movement keys. This means that your building keys are very close to your fingers which are resting on your keyboard.

# Panic Walls and Ramps to Access Areas

If you do happen to get caught up in heavy fire, you can simply drop a wall in front of you in order to protect yourself. People are calling this short-term cover "panic walls". It's a great way to create quick cover so you can retreat in time. You can also choose to stay and fight by adding a ramp to the wall. This way you will be able to walk up the ramp towards the top of the wall. Your opponent won't expect to see you. This way you can get the jump on him.

Third-person view helps a lot here as it makes it easier for you to view your opponent. But it isn't the same for them as they won't be able to see you. You can also build ramps towards areas that are not accessible. This could be towards the top of buildings and other opponents forts. This can help you to locate a proper vantage point as well as invade the enemy's fort. Ramping high up beside someone else's fort will give you the high ground advantage on them.

# Chapter 8: Strategies to Go from Noob to Pro Quickly

## 1. Take Cover

Avoid running out in the open when moving from one location to another. Use buildings, mountains, and trees for cover. Someone spotting you can lead to an unexpected gunfight.

## 2. Entering the Circle

Don't always assume that the rest of the players are already inside the circle once you have arrived there. It is possible that most of them are still making their way over there. Be alert as they could approach from behind you and take you out. You rather anticipate their moves and pick them off from inside the circle.

## 3. Wear Headphones

As mentioned earlier, it is strongly

recommended that you wear headphones. This is a great way to monitor footsteps and other nearby battles. Sounds in Fortnite Battle Royale feel louder than other shooters. Use this to your advantage.

## 4. Looting Buildings

Resources and weapons seem to spawn more frequently in commonly populated areas and buildings. You can find some great weapons here, but you will most probably encounter other attacking players. It's high-risk high reward. If you feel up to the challenge and the risk is worth it, then you should go for it. Otherwise, focus on looting less populated areas.

## 5. Doors

There are simple mind games involved in leaving doors open and closed. It's best to close a door when you enter a room. That way, people won't think that you already entered the room.

You can use this element of surprise to your advantage and get the jump on any unexpected intruders. Also leaving the door open as you leave will make people suspect that someone is in the room when they are not!

# Chapter 9: Ultimate Fortnite Challenges

Fortnite Challenges are fun objectives that were added to the game around Season 3. These challenges become available once you purchase a Battle Pass for a season. There are new challenges each week. Completing them will help you to earn XP. Earning XP can assist you in upgrading your tiers which can lead to more rewards and V-Bucks.

Weekly Challenges is one of the main reasons why you should consider getting a Battle Pass. They are fun and rewarding. Some may have a treasure hunt element to them. Basically, you will need to search areas for a specific item or chests. Other challenges will focus on specific tasks like destroying opponents structures or harvesting a specific amount of materials.

The Fortnite community is also responsible for coming up with their own challenges. An example would be a challenge where you must only use the first weapon that you pick up for the entire game. This creates a new level of difficulty for the player. Most of which end up live streaming the results. These challenges are a great way to keep the game fresh.

# Conclusion

Thank you again for reading this book. I really hope that you enjoyed reading it and most of all I hope that it was able to offer you a better understanding of Fortnite Battle Royale.

All of the most important tips that you will need to be successful in the game can be found in this book. It is now up to you to put whatever you have learned from this book to the ultimate test. You may stumble at first, but keep trying and you will eventually become a pro.

Have an awesome time playing Fortnite Battle Royale and hope to see you on the battlefield soon.

38087597R00026

Made in the USA
Columbia, SC
03 December 2018